simplified.

A Real-Life Guide to Organizing Your Space and Saving Your Sanity

By Stephanie B. Sikora

Copyright © 2018 by Stephanie B. Sikora

All rights reserved. No part of this book may be reproduced in any form or by any means—electronic, mechanical, photocopying, scanning or otherwise—without written permission from the author, except by a reviewer who may quote

Amazon Digital Services LLC

Printed in the United States of America

ISBN: 9781731383761

Table of Contents

Praise v
Foreword vii
Introduction 1
Chapter 1: My Story 5
    Not Your Average Professional Organizer 5
    A Gift I Couldn't Waste 6
    Hard-Wired to Organize 11
    Clutter, Stress, and Purpose 13
    The Joy of Purging.. 15
Chapter 2: The Truth About Clutter 19
    Life, Cluttered 19
    I'm Cluttered, You're Cluttered, We're All Cluttered 20
    Cluttered Homes, Cluttered Brains................... 21
    We're All Wired Differently 23
    This Is Your Brain on Clutter 27
Chapter 3: Areas of Impact 35
    The Clutter Impact Assessment 36
    Relationship Clutter 45
    Health Clutter 48
    "My Kitchen Makes Me Crazy!"........................ 49
    Money Clutter.. 51
    Time Clutter 58

Chapter 4: Simple Isn't Always Easy 61
  Barriers to Change 62
  Getting Started 64
  Clutter vs. Hoarding 66
  Three Steps to Less Stress in Your Space 69
Chapter 5: Simplify 73
  The Simplest, Hardest Thing 73
  Simplifying Can Be Simple 76
  Sentimental Objects 78
  Kids' Toys 79
Chapter 6: Systematize 83
  The Magic of a System 83
  Real Systems (In the Real World) 85
  Creating Your Zones 88
  Frequency of Use 89
  Find Your Flow 90
Chapter 7: Sustain 97
  Bringing Stuff Back In 98
  Parting Ways with Stuff (Again) 100
  Maintaining Systems 101
Chapter 8: Sanity 105
Chapter 9: What's Next 107
Epilogue 113
Acknowledgements 115
Notes 117

Praise

"I love how Stephanie used her background in healthcare to help families get their households up and running more efficiently. She breaks it into three simple steps that are easy to follow and truly get results. She has helped me shift my mindset around being organized— from a scary and overwhelming process to a simple process of slowing down to create practical systems that work with your current habits and lifestyle. I love her encouragement to start small (with just your junk drawer) to build up confidence and momentum. Once I started purging, it really became fun and the more I got rid of the lighter I felt. I can't wait to start tackling some bigger areas of my house with her resources in my back pocket!"

Lindsay McCarthy, Co-Author of *The Miracle Morning for Parents and Families*,
Co-Creator of www.GratefulParent.com

"simplified. is a great guide for moms who are looking to slow things down. Stephanie offers practical and doable strategies allowing you to feel less overwhelmed and create a life that is not so busy and stressful. This is a must read for moms who want more time for what matters most in life."

Kristen Race, Ph.D., Author of *Mindful Parenting*,
Creator of The Mindful Life™ Method

"Stephanie Sikora is a genius. Combining her background in the medical field, her knowledge of neuropsychology, psychology, and experience with human behavior, she offers a fresh perspective on creating systems for your home that will help your day to run smoother, become more enjoyable, and with much less hassle. Not only has Stephanie helped me in my personal home and worked through the process of creating some crucial systems, she's also be an incredible catalyst for personal change among my coaching community. Our community members have begun to value their spaces, create systems, enjoy their homes and environments, and make lasting improvements to their daily habits and systems. What Stephanie shares changes lives in such a pleasantly unexpected way. Take the time for yourself so that you can experience the same things we have!"

Erica Powell, Founder of Erica Powell & Co.
Lifestyle Architects

Foreword

As I was launching my book, *Mommy Burnout*, I was fortunate to meet Stephanie at a book discussion. After I was through speaking, Stephanie knew there was alignment between my message about stress and the effects it has on parenting and her message about stress and the role that clutter and lack of organization plays in parenting and other parts of our lives. As she started talking about the inability to be present, fully engaged and focused because we feel so out of control in our homes, offices or bedrooms I knew that we were speaking the same language.

Stephanie is one of the most qualified people I can imagine to have written Simplified. Her experience counseling medical professionals with burnout in the workplace and creating systems in the medical field to help with efficiency were great experiences to prepare her for becoming a mother and realizing that in order to experience motherhood to its fullest she would need to create similar systems in the home or she would never fully experience peace in parenthood. Her stories about how we tell our kids to wait and give us a minute because we have to clean up are all too relatable. By the time I was done reading the book, I actually felt excited and motivated to declutter and get organized in order to regain my joy in parenting... and in simply just coming home.

Simplified, also made a compelling case for the way that our brains are activated when we see chaos. The chaos of our kids' toys, our piles of papers and dishes in the sink cause us to go into a state of stress before we even say a word. I have experienced this stress myself and had the great fortune of having Stephanie come to my home office. I explained to her that the piles of papers, sticky notes, and to-do lists in my office were causing me to avoid my space. I built an office for writing and being creative and a few years later was so buried in clutter that I started working out of the kitchen island. Stephanie came in and helped me create a system that made sense. She helped me go through piles that were taking up physical and emotional space in my life. Working out of the space is now a totally different experience, one that I actually look forward to instead of dread.

However, now that I have read this whole book I realize that I have the inspiration (my peace and sanity) and the tools (the steps in this book) to go through the rest of my house to create this in other spaces like my kids' bedrooms and playroom. I have been convinced that investing the time to do that will give us all the gift of being more relaxed as a family so we can focus on the things that matter. I truly didn't understand until I read this book how my inner desire to be a more organized mom was going to be attained. It's more than just cleaning up on Saturday afternoon, it's about creating systems that make sense and teaching these systems to my family.

I hope you will enjoy Simplified as much as I did and start using the tools in here. Lack of organization and clutter adds to burnout and stress and Stephanie has written the book on how we can all break free from too much stuff and get back to doing things we love.

Dr. Sheryl Gonzalez-Ziegler,
Author of *Mommy Burnout*

Introduction

This book is intended to make your life perfect. By the time you finish this book, your home, life, and relationships will be flawless.

I'm totally kidding! I wanted to get that out of the way now so we can let go of the idea that this book is about creating something perfect. This book is actually about how we can create the space, time, energy, money, and awareness to spend more time doing what means the most to us. At my core, this is what means the most to me—helping people connect with themselves and one another.

Our world only gets busier and more distracting, but our home environments and our minds don't need to be. This is not just another book about organizing your home. This is about creating life systems that help us to slow down and not work so hard every day to simply clothe, feed and bathe our offspring, let alone ourselves. This book is about simplifying our lives and creating systems that last and work even with those who are not as motivated as we are to keep things tidy.

simplified.

I never thought I would write a book. For most of my life, I was a "should" kind of girl. I "should" run for student government. I "should" go to the school that offered me the scholarship. I "should" follow the stable path with a job. I "should" have a child at this time. On and on it went.

But then a few years ago, I attended a course through Stanford titled Cultivating Compassion Training. During class, my instructor told me, "Stop 'shoulding' all over yourself!" And she was right! Nowhere in my list of "shoulds" was "write a book." It scared me to do something that was not a "should". I risked exposing my deepest thoughts and life stories. But maybe I "should" share my story and my passion. I get so excited about helping people understand how our space—physical, digital, and mental—impacts the way we show up in life as individuals, partners, parents, professionals, pet owners, and more.

People tell me they see my face light up when I talk about our spaces and how they affect us. Now, I see no reason why I *shouldn't* write this book! I'm sharing my story and my passion to help others create spaces, homes, and lives that give them more energy, time, finances, and awareness. It's time to stop allowing our homes to deplete us of these resources so we can

Introduction

start living lives full of connection and meaning. An ongoing study conducted at Harvard for over seventy-five years concluded that connection with others is the greatest indicator of longevity, yet we are becoming more and more disconnected from one another and ourselves. Living a life that is a little more simplified is a step to start reconnecting to what matters most.

CHAPTER 1

My Story

Not Your Average Professional Organizer

I'm not your average Professional Organizer. Actually, I don't even like to think of myself as a "Professional Organizer." I know the work that I'm fortunate enough to do goes much deeper than a pretty closet.

When most people think of organization, they think of having a perfect space that's decked out with expensive bins and labels. Everything is color coordinated and never out of place. Who actually lives like that—for more than five minutes? Not this mom with two little girls, a very hairy golden retriever, and a husband who thinks his piles on the floor are a good system. Ha!

To me, organization is not about having a perfect space. It's about creating a space that's clear, calm, and allows me to feel less crazy and distracted! As long as I can remember, I've always enjoyed rearranging my home. As a pre-teen, I would tear apart my room and organize it for fun. I'm lucky I had already established some solid friendships before this phase. Nerd alert! But it wasn't until the universe completely changed my path that I began to see my passion for order and clear spaces differently.

A Gift I Couldn't Waste

On a Monday in January, 2017, my life changed. I'd been working in healthcare for fifteen years. I earned separate graduate degrees in Clinical Exercise Physiology and Healthcare Leadership. I thought I would be in healthcare until retirement. I liked the steady paycheck and benefits of a corporate job. Crazy, I know!

Well, on this particular Monday, I was told my role and my department were being eliminated. That was it. I no longer had a job. I walked out of the building on the phone with my husband in tears. Next thing I knew, I was home full-time with my kiddos. It was a shock to my system to say the least. Not only was I grieving the loss of a career, I was trying to figure out how I was going to do this whole stay-at-home-mom thing. It was not an easy transition. Not that I didn't want to be home with my kids, it was just a major adjustment. My first reaction was to find another secure (or not-so-secure) corporate job, because I believed that was what I *should* do. But something deep in my soul was telling me, "No!" As scary as it was, I listened.

A few weeks into this transition process, I caught myself in a pattern of running around, picking up toys, and telling the kids to put their things away—basically running in circles all day. I was exhausted just from taking care of all the things we needed to do each day in our home and life. My kiddos would ask me to play or to color, and I would respond with, "One second, let mommy just put this stuff away," or, "I'll be right over as soon as I get the kitchen cleaned."

One day not too far into this new phase of my life, my oldest daughter, who was four at the time, looked at me and said, "But mom, you *never* finish and come play with us." Insert knife into heart.

Really? Is *that* how I want my kids to remember their childhood? How I want them to remember me? Is *this* the life I want for myself?

simplified.

There *had* to be a better way to keep me from losing my mind, make the most of the time with my kids, and show up as the mom and wife I wanted to be.

Something clicked—this time at home with my kids was truly a gift, and there I was wasting it by driving myself (and everyone else) crazy trying to keep the house in order. The organization was partly to maintain a clean, calm house, but that wasn't the real reason for my obsession. The fact is, I'm hard-wired to want things in order, and it's hard for me to be present, happy, or calm when they're *not* in order. Maybe you can relate—I'm the type of person who can't sit and relax after dinner until the kitchen is cleaned up. I appreciate it when my husband offers to do the dishes, but then I sit there and think, *Thanks, honey, that's so sweet! Can you do them now, not tomorrow?*

I felt like I wasted my days trying to keep my house in order, instead of spending quality time with my kiddos or taking time to do something for myself. I realized I was living the definition of insanity—doing the same thing repeatedly but expecting a different result. I used to run around picking up toys only to find a mess just moments later—again, with two small kids this was normal life. I have heard many moms refer to this as the "hamster wheel" of motherhood. Heck, no! If I'm going to go for a run, I'm going to hit the trail with a girlfriend, then grab a delicious brunch where I over-caffeinate and overindulge in something yummy, then keep going back and forth about whether I should have a mimosa.

Deep down, I wanted to be patient and present with my kids, and (let me be honest) not have my house resemble an explosion! I wanted to have more time to do things for myself. I wanted to rekindle my great connection with my husband that went beyond managing our house and parenting our kids. I wanted to live in a space that energized me.

I'm the CFO, CEO, and COO of our household, and I wanted to have an efficient organization where time with my family is our mission! While we're on acronyms, I have to say that my husband is the CTO—Chief Travel Officer. As a world traveler, he's always been the best travel planner and travel is a big part of our family time. We don't always get to go on extravagant vacations, but he plans the best trips when we do get away. Thanks, honey!

I think my new obsession to keep our house in order was also my way of managing the stress of my new situation. I wanted to control *something.* This transition was not easy on my family or my marriage. Prior to losing my job, I had a six-figure paycheck with amazing healthcare benefits. Overnight, we reduced our household income by sixty percent. I *needed* to work. We had just moved into a new, bigger house so my mother-in-law could live with us and help with our girls. There were a lot of people depending on my husband and I to keep our house and our family intact. Part of me was holding out hope that a secure job would come along...and part of me was hoping it wouldn't. As hard as it was on our family, I felt compelled to do something different. Different than what was safe, reasonable, and secure.

I remember sitting at the desk in our house one afternoon, feeling defeated. I'd just read an email response from a company I'd been talking to about helping them to expand to my area. Then I got a text from a former colleague about another potential job. It turned out neither opportunity was going to pan out. As I sat there feeling sorry for myself, I remembered reading an article by Shawn Achor about taking small bouts of stress and using them to drive you forward. Suddenly, I had a fire inside of me—a mix of panic, defeat, and most of all, motivation. I thought, *I'm going to do my own thing.*

For me, entrepreneurship didn't happen overnight. Starting a business overlapped with my personal journey to stop the chaos of managing our home. I wanted to help other moms who were struggling with managing their households, who wanted more than just exhausting themselves each day just to get everything done. But I didn't really *launch* my business, I *evolved* it. I don't even remember how I told my husband about my business idea—I was in a completely different state of mind. Fortunately, he didn't shut me down. Although I think he secretly hoped I'd come to my senses and rejoin corporate America. I didn't. And I'm *glad* I didn't. Even though self-employment comes without a safety net, my previous career gave me ninety percent of what I'd need to succeed in my new reality. I just didn't realize it yet.

Hard-Wired to Organize

During my career in healthcare, one of my roles was to coach physicians experiencing work-related burnout. I learned a lot about the brain and the impact of burnout on all aspects of our lives. When I started my business, I began to see so many connections between burnout related to work and stress in our physical space. Much of the overwhelm my clients were seeking my services for in their homes contributed to the burnout they were feeling in life.

In addition to coaching physicians to focus on their own wellness, I also worked on improving clinical spaces. My work centered around implementing a method called Process Improvement. Process Improvement originally started in the automotive industry, but was later adopted into healthcare. Basically, I would look at physical spaces and processes, evaluating them for opportunities to eliminate waste and improve efficiencies, and identify ways to save time, money and energy. For example, one of my assignments was to look at a procedural room where patients underwent minor surgical procedures. I mapped out the steps a surgical tech or nurse took throughout performing the procedure—how many steps they took to find each medical instrument, and how long each step took. My goal was to reduce the overall number of steps, ultimately reducing the time the procedure took, and thereby reducing the risk of infection, improving the quality of care, and improving the patient's outcome.

One day during a typical frenzied "get the house in order because mom is going to lose her you-know-what" session, a lightbulb went off—my kitchen was just like an operating room. There were knives, but no blood, thank goodness! My kitchen had various areas—cooking, dishwashing, lunch preparation, etc. I could optimize each area to reduce the overall amount of work I had to do performing these tasks! I had been professionally trained to look at a space and identify the inefficiencies. I loved doing this! My brain loved it, and my house became my next project. *Mwahahaha!* (Insert husband shaking his head.)

It was time for me to step off the hamster wheel and start applying these principles to other high traffic, highly stressed areas of our home. I evaluated where things were kept. Did they need to be *there*, or was there a better home for them? Better yet, did we even *need* them? Where the pre-teen girl would have previously organized a space so that it looked "cute," or the mom in me would feel like it "should" look like a Pinterest post, I started looking at our spaces and identifying systems that made us more efficient and our lives less hectic. It was more about function than aesthetics, though. I would do a dance inside when our spaces functioned well *and* looked good. I was on a new mission to make our life and home less chaotic.

Clutter, Stress, and Purpose

Before I could implement effective systems in our house that actually lasted, I had to simplify our belongings. I was seriously looking at everything in our house and considering whether or not we needed it. As I addressed the different areas in my home, not from a place of *stress* but with a sense of *purpose*, I realized that the chemistry of my brain was changing.

You know that dopamine rush or high some people get when they purchase something, especially when it's on sale? I was getting that same feeling from letting go of stuff. It felt so good! With each item tossed or sold, I felt freer and lighter. My kids started getting nervous anytime they saw something on the porch for pick up. I knew I had to be careful, or my kids would become hoarders, hiding things in their closets to avoid being purged!

This process of simplifying our space and removing the items that did not serve a purpose or add value to our lives continued for about six months. It felt great, and my family started to notice the benefits—less stuff to pick up, less distraction, and more freedom! We also started being very thoughtful about what we brought *in* to our house.

Just as Cait Flanders shares her experiment with a one year shopping ban in *The Year of Less*, we became "mindful consumers." I think our new budget restrictions helped with that, but it also made us more aware of what we used to buy unnecessarily. Although the UPS man may have taken it personally when he was no longer at my doorstep every day, I realized how often I'd clicked on the Amazon app and added whatever item it was that I thought I "needed." It's not that we were previously buying extravagant things, but I wouldn't hesitate to grab an item that we "could use in our house" or a "fun" game or activity for my kiddos. Now I was more mindful, realizing how much I could get by without. It actually became a challenge I set for myself. How many days could I go without purchasing something?

By now you might be envisioning a minimalist living in a bare room wearing a burlap sack. But trust me, we still had *plenty* of stuff in our house, and my kids had *plenty* of toys on the playroom floor—we just had less of it.

The Joy of Purging

Purging our home of unwanted clutter helped me:

- stop the insanity of trying to keep everything tidy

- manage the stress of my career transition, giving me a sense of control

- channel my previously career-focused energy in a new direction

I remember a day when my then four year-old asked me to sit with her at the craft table and do some art with her. She loves to draw. We sat at her table, and she used a blue crayon to draw the sky. I looked at her and saw how focused and happy she was. In that moment of calm, I made a silent promise to make this my priority. I thought to myself, *Why don't I make more time to do this?* Just then, she looked up at me and said, "Mom, you are not coloring!" I was so focused on her and taking in this moment—this uninterrupted, quality time with my daughter. Not that we sat around coloring and singing kumbaya all day! But since I had started simplifying our space, I had more time with my family and more time for myself.

One summer day, my husband and I were playing with the kids in the backyard, swinging them on this spider web-like swing. *Why didn't we take this path of simplifying our home sooner?*

Years before, when we first considered having a second child, we talked to our friends about how far apart their children were, wanting to create an ideal age gap for ours. Our kids ended up being twenty-eight months apart, which has turned out really well. They're as close as best friends, which means one minute they're playing together and fighting over a toy the next.

What was most significant for me when creating better systems in our home was not how our spaces changed, but how *I* changed. I started to show up differently for my family and for myself. I started to slow down. I started to be more present and more patient. During a recent visit with my sister-in-law, my girls were arguing over the same toy. Although it goes against a lot of parenting books, I usually tell them to figure it out on their own. Most of the time they can. My sister-in-law looked at me surprised, and said, "You're so patient with them." That's not always the case, but when my environment is clean and simple, *I'm* more calm and patient. Moments like this will teach my kids how to handle adversity and challenges in life. When I was preoccupied with trying keep the house in order all the time, I missed these opportunities—cue me yelling and threatening toy removal (AKA, an ineffective parenting strategy).

I'm a firm believer that the universe has a way of leading us down the right path at the right time (although secretly, I wish I could always be in control). But what if I could help lead other families down this path without a life-altering event? What if I could help them create a home environment that fosters improved relationships, efficiencies, and the ability to be present? Maybe this was the path the universe was guiding me down—the process in our own home just prepared me for it.

It's been such a gift to be invited into so many homes to help others create a space that allows them to be more present, healthy, focused, kind, patient, financially aware, and efficient —and those are just a few of the words my clients have shared with me. When I work with people in their homes, I capture before and after images of their spaces. What I wish I could *really* capture in those images is how the individual transforms as a result of the space transformation. *That's* where the true magic happens.

Summary:

- We are all wired differently. For some of us, it's difficult to focus and relax when our space is in disarray. There is actually a stress response in our brain that causes this.

- Too much stuff and too few systems make us feel like we're constantly trying to keep up with all of our responsibilities.

CHAPTER 2

The Truth About Clutter

Life, Cluttered

Imagine...You walk into your house after a long day at work. The place looks like the scene of a crime—dishes, papers, clothes, and toys exploded everywhere! *What the heck happened? I cleaned the house right before I left, and now it's a hot mess!* You feel anxious and stressed. Instead of giving your kids and husband a hug, you let out a huge sigh, roll your eyes, and scream on the inside—maybe on the outside, too. Sound familiar?

simplified.

I'm Cluttered, You're Cluttered, We're All Cluttered

I define clutter as stuff that just sits around, no longer serving a purpose, bringing you joy, or adding value to your life. This could be anything from a few stacks of papers to old clothes piled to the ceiling. We all have different thresholds for clutter, but the pattern of clutter frustration is actually pretty universal.

I've worked with many individuals and families, spoken to women's groups, and taught courses on the topic of clutter and its impact on our lives. When I meet with clients or speak to groups, I usually start the conversation with the following questions:

"Have you ever walked into a messy room or looked around your physical space and groaned at the amount of stuff and lack of organization?"

A resounding, "YES!"

"Is there a space in your home or work environment that gives you a sense of anxiety when you enter it?" They all nod their heads in agreement.

"What does it look like for you when you experience that anxiety?"

They respond with, "I feel stressed," "I get overwhelmed," or "I'm grumpy with my spouse. I snap at my kids."

"And how does that make you feel?" I ask.

"So guilty. Like I'm a bad parent and a control freak."

I continue the conversation with my clients. I say, "What would it mean to you if you organized this space?"

"That would be a huge relief! I'd be so much less stressed."

It can be difficult leading people down a path that brings out these emotions, but I find value in helping them realize that they are NOT bad parents, partners, or negative people. Often we don't realize the way we're showing up and interacting with others has a lot to do with our environment. When our space is cluttered or disorganized, it affects other aspects of our lives—relationships, health, finances, and time management.

Cluttered Homes, Cluttered Brains

As a Clinical Exercise Physiologist, I spent many years helping individuals create new behaviors to improve their health. I worked with heart patients who had recently experienced a heart attack or some other cardiac event, as well as high-risk patients headed down the same path if they didn't make a change. I knew what goes into changing their behaviors and which puzzle pieces need to be in place for true change to occur.

When you're struggling to make changes in one aspect of life, it's often beneficial to look at how your environment could be holding you back. I never realized what a big role our environment plays until I started doing this type of work in people's homes. Clients tell me, "I really want to make a career change and start my own business, but I need to get my house in order first," or, "I need to move forward with my divorce, but I can't find the strength until I get rid of all of this stuff."

I have a client, Amy, who's a mom of three boys. She's a relatively organized person. But sometimes life gets too hectic, and we just need some help making the time to get some good systems in place for day-to-day responsibilities in our home.

Amy had taken some time away from her career to raise her sons. When we meet, she talked ambitiously about her goals to return to her career—or start something new. After we'd worked together for several weeks, she started to notice that the cluttered spaces in her house were part of the reason she couldn't move forward. Once we started clearing the spaces, she noticed how free she felt. When she had a better handle on her house and her life, she could plan the next step in her career.

This scenario is pretty common, illustrating the power our space has to hold us back. Think about the last time you sat down to work on a project, whether it was doing your taxes or helping your child with her homework. Did you need to clear off your table before you could truly focus? I know I work much more efficiently when I clear off my desk first. When I'm in my kitchen, and dishes cover over the counter (or scraps of craft paper litter the floor), it's like loud music is playing in my head. I can't focus. I need to clear the space—and turn down the volume of the music. Clear counters? *Ahhh*. Much quieter in my head.

We're All Wired Differently

Let's face it—we're all wired differently. There are some people who are actually *more* creative in a space that's *not* tidy. Some people can function with the volume turned *way* up. Take Steve Jobs. Clearly a creative person who accomplished great things. But his work space was always cluttered with papers and books. It amazes me how someone who had such a cluttered workspace could create such amazing things. Things that were so simple—the first iPod had just one button! Unfortunately, I think Steve Jobs was unique in that he was able to make magic in a chaotic space. Most people can't. We have a way lower threshold for clutter and chaos. This different wiring can definitely pose some challenges at home. One person may need things tidy while the other is oblivious—or as I describe my husband, "clutter-blind."

I spend a lot of time in my clients' homes. Within the first few minutes of entering, I hear how their spaces are impacting their marriage or parenting. I don't even ask! They dive right into how one partner feels about it versus the other, or how they get so frustrated with their kids.

My client, Carrie, has two daughters. They're totally different about how they keep their rooms. Her older daughter kept things tidy and follows the rules on her responsibility chart. Her younger daughter has no problem with the floor covered with stuffed animals and clothes. Carrie kept getting frustrated with her. She always followed her around the house to pick up after her. This was *not* how she wanted her kids to remember her!

We talked it through. She learned that each of our brains is wired differently. When we understand this simple fact, we can be a little more patient when dealing with kids or spouses who aren't as interested in keeping things in order. I'm not saying you should give your disorganized child a free pass. It's just helpful when you can recognize your differences. Think about what might motivate them to keep their room tidy or pick up their toys. Yes, there are benefits to keeping our spaces in order, but it becomes a strain when we're always nagging our children. It's exhausting. Trust me, I know.

Carrie's younger daughter still has the responsibility of keeping her room tidy, but we created a system that works for how her mind operates (more on this later). We talked about her daughter's desk. Carrie thought it was just a mess, but it was actually an obstacle course she had set up for her dolls! Carried only figured this out when she stopped judging and started asking.

At the most basic level, we all desire to have a sense of order. Even those who have piles on the floor have some order associated with them. At one of the groups I spoke to, there was one brave guy in the

simplified.

audience who raised his hand. He shared how he and his wife were both tidy people, but they each had different approaches to how they cleaned.

The husband said, "We both like the kitchen clean, but my wife likes the dishes done immediately after dinner. I like the dishes done, too, but why can't they wait until the next day?"

The entire audience of women laughed, threw their heads back and laughed. It's a perfect example of people's different methods of keeping things neat. We have different thresholds for what we can tolerate—and for what triggers a stress response in our brain. I explained to the man in the audience that the full sink most likely stressed out his wife. It wasn't a criticism of him—her stress response trigger was just different than his. I don't think he ran right home and did the dishes after he heard my words (I am *not* a miracle worker). But he definitely saw the situation differently afterward.

Even if we can't control others' behavior, we can still maintain calm inside. And we must. So much is at stake! I've always tried to be a good mom. I try to feed my kids well, limit their screen time, and teach them good manners. But isn't all that negated if I'm not present enough to play with them? To be patient and focused when they need me? Our kids grow up confident and kind to those around them when they feel appreciated, noticed, and loved. Like most (if not all) moms, If I want to be there for my kids, I need to have my space in some kind of order. Now we know *why*.

This Is Your Brain on Clutter

What happens in our brain when our space is cluttered? What happens when our space is clear?

Surrounded by clutter, we're stressed, grumpy, and less present. Sadly, the fight or flight alarm that helped us survive during our caveman days is now triggered often in our day-to-day lives. This "alarm" part of our brain goes off for much smaller stressors, such as to-do lists, traffic, and social media. The more often we trigger this part of our brain, the more automatic a response it becomes for us. Over time, we literally halt our ability to be focused, rational, and compassionate—all traits that have a home in the "smart" part of our brain.

Participants in a Princeton University study underwent brain scans while viewing images of clutter. The study confirmed that clutter triggers that alarm part of our brain![1] Get triggered too often, and you exhaust your mind into a chronic stress response. Clear our space,

simplified.

and we get triggered less. This literally restores our brain power.

Research shows that our brains are not equipped for today's technology-ubiquitous world. Our brains were not designed for multi-tasking. I always used to think I was a "good" multitasker. The more I've learned, the more I've realized I'm actually *less* effective when I do two things at once. I've since changed my routines to create more systems that allow me to focus on one task at a time. I do one thing efficiently and move on to the next thing. This saves me so much time and brain power! Sometimes, I find myself falling back into my old ways and trying to do three or four things at a time, running around wondering, *Wait! What was I doing over here?* No bueno! But it happens.

Look at it this way—your brain is an energy bank. You only have so much energy in it to use each day. When we can't find something or easily identify where to put it away, we deplete that energy. It's a mundane, daily task! You're racking up exorbitant ATM fees to withdraw five bucks!. It's not worth it! David Levitin, author of *The Organized Mind*, calls this brain drain.

Think about the frenzied state of mind you're in when you're running late to get to work or drop the kids off at school. You dart around the house, searching for your keys, snapping at everyone along the way. This is *not* a good way to start your day—you've wasted a large amount of your brain's energy, you've made yourself even later getting out the door, you've triggered a stress response that raises your blood pressure, and worst of all, you're making your spouse, kids, and pets want to stay as far away from you as possible!

On the flip side, when you have things in order, you use little to no energy to find your keys, wallet, glasses, etc., making it easier to get out the door on time. You reserve your brain's energy for the important things, such as working on a project that requires your creativity, being patient when your kid needs you to listen, or even conserving energy for yourself at the end of a long day.

Brain Energy Bank When You Lack Systems

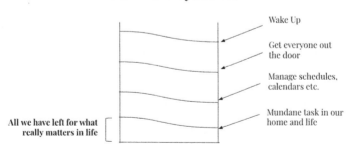

simplified.

Brain Energy Bank After Simplifying and Creating Systems

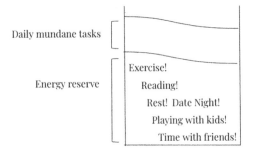

While writing this chapter, I had to schedule my older daughter's tonsil and adenoid removal surgery. About six days post-op, I went over to my sister-in-law's to help clear out some spaces in her house. I was pleasantly surprised she wanted me to help her out. Let's just say, she isn't the most organized person. She tends to lose things...all the time. Even the most disorganized people still want to have some kind of order in their lives!

My daughter came along and laid on her couch with some popsicles while I tackled a few of my sister-in-law's spaces. We got some areas in order, which left her feeling excited. Later that night, I was awakened by my daughter to find a pool of bright red blood in her bed. I knew this was a common consequence of having your tonsils out, but I remembered the surgeon's words, "No amount of blood is normal." I rushed her to the emergency room as quickly as I could.

My husband stayed home with my younger daughter. On the way, I called my sister-in-law and asked her to meet me there. Without hesitation, she agreed. When my daughter and I arrived at the hospital, my sister-in-law was already waiting for us. She does live a mile closer to the hospital, but I was still surprised by how fast she got there. When I shared my appreciation and surprise at her promptness, she replied, "Well, I knew where everything was so I was able to get out the door quickly. My keys, shoes, purse. It was all so easy for me to find!" She didn't have to waste any (limited) energy in the middle of the night and was able to arrive quickly to be with me and my daughter, for which I was so grateful.

That's why I do what I do, and it's what I hope I can do for more people. Help them *not* to miss the little moments in life and have more energy for the big ones when people count on them the most. Even if you're not running out the door for an emergency, but just trying to get through a normal day, clutter and chaos can drain you so quickly. In my opinion, this is completely avoidable. Think about how it affects our children. How is a cluttered or chaotic environment affecting their learning ability at school?

My husband is a middle school counselor. As a young man, he planned on going to law school until he did a summer internship and realized he wanted to help kids *before* they got caught up in the judicial system. He changed career paths and went to graduate school to become a school counselor. He amazes me with the impact he has on the kids. We talk about the students every day and about how important their home environment is. He tells me stories of kids who don't show up for school. He and the police officer assigned to his school hop in the cruiser and head over to the kid's house. He's so sad to see the chaos of these kids' homes. "Total mess" doesn't get halfway there. They have such an uphill battle before they can even think about school.

Extreme situations? Sure. You might be thinking, *My house isn't that bad.* Now, I'm sure it's not the same as what my husband walks into some days. But I work with many upper-middle class kids who have everything they could ever want. All too often, having so much stuff (and such lack of order) is chaotic for their brains. The volume is too loud. It triggers that negative "alarm" and shuts off the "smart" part of their brain that allows them to be creative and focused. I see a correlation between clutter and children with ADHD and ADD. But if we keep our homes clear and organized, and if we follow a routine, our kids can focus on one thing at a time without constantly feeling distracted.

A client of mine, Michelle, has a daughter in middle school who asked to work with me as her Christmas present. I was touched—and I have to say, she was one of the most polite and mature sixth graders I have ever met. We spent the day working in her room, and she shared how much she disliked having so much stuff cluttering her space. She told her mom, "I love you, and I appreciate all the stuff you buy for me, but I don't need it." It was actually having the *opposite* effect that her mom had intended. Instead of bringing her joy, it made her anxious. She couldn't function with the volume dial turned way up. Her mom was open and completely understood. I'm fortunate to work with clients like Michelle and help them realize that they're not crazy, uptight, or OCD. I get to show them they're not alone. Neither are you.

Summary:

- Clutter and chaos in our environment triggers a stress response in our brain.

simplified.

- We are all wired differently and have different thresholds for clutter and chaos in our environment. Clutter and lack of organization impact our lives, causing frustration, lost money and time, overlooked health goals, even resentment and tension in a relationship.
- Your environment is at the core of most behavior change models. If you're not progressing, take a step back to assess your environment to reveal what's preventing you from moving forward.

CHAPTER 3

Areas of Impact

When I was pregnant with my first child, I read a lot of pregnancy books. Maybe all of them! I feel bad for my second daughter. I don't think I read a single book the second time around. For her, I relied on my memory, which was pretty rusty! But I do remember all of the books agreeing on one thing: babies cry because of *overstimulation*. Spaces with too much going on overstimulate infants' brains, making them feel overwhelmed and upset.

Not so different from the way messy spaces affect adults, is it? Our brains never change. Our cluttered, chaotic environment overstimulates us, causing us to cry, scream at our children, or hide in a closet with a glass of wine. That was the case for me. The

simplified.

overstimulation impacted everything and everyone around me, beginning with my own sanity.

The Clutter Impact Assessment

Before we get into *how* you can create clear and calm spaces in your home and your life, I want you to take this quick and easy **Clutter Impact Assessment**. Remember the quizzes you used to take in *Cosmopolitan* magazine? It's just like that! I created this to help people see how their spaces impact different aspects of their and their families' lives. The Clutter Impact Assessment is a fun tool intended to help you see the true impact of clutter and chaos, highlight the potential benefits of simplifying your life, and heighten your awareness of opportunities to create a simple, more calming environment. If you don't like to do math, you can also take quiz online at: www.lifemadesimpleathome.com/resources.

Answer each question on a scale of 1-4. Just keep track of how many #1's, #2's, #3's, and #4's you have.

Areas of Impact

1. On a scale of 1-4, how much stress and tension do you feel when you look at the physical space in your home?
    1. No stress
    2. Some stress
    3. A fair amount of stress—I'm reminded each day when I walk in the door.
    4. Stressed to the max—I cringe when I look around!

   Answer: ____ *4*

2. On a scale of 1-4, how would you rate the effect that clutter and disorganization have on your mood?
    1. Disorganization has no impact on me at all—I'm always polite, regardless.
    2. I can be a little short with my family when things are out of order.
    3. I often lose my temper when I go in circles trying to tidy my house
    4. It's best everyone just steers clear of me!

   Answer: ____ *2/3*

simplified.

3. On a scale of 1-4, how much does disorganization in your home impact your relationships and communication with your family?

    1. Not at all. We're all on the same page with how we keep our house organized and tidy.

    2. We have some differing opinions, but we're able to talk about them.

    3. Disorganization has created tension between my partner/kids and myself.

    4. It's one of the greatest points of frustration and it's led to many disagreements.

Answer: 3

4. On a scale of 1-4, how much money do you think you have lost due to a lack of organizational systems in your home?

    1. We've actually saved lots of money with our systems!

    2. I have had to re-purchase a few items because we couldn't find them or forgot we already owned them.

Areas of Impact

3. I'm always running out to buy more stuff because I can't find anything!

4. I don't even want to think about how much we're wasting due to lack of organization!

Answer: _2_

5. On a scale of 1-4, how much time do you think you have lost due to a lack of organizational systems in your home?

   1. My streamlined processes in my home make me super-efficient with my daily activities (e.g. preparing meals, cleaning, getting my kids out the door).

   2. I have some systems in place that help me save time, but I can see additional opportunities to streamline.

   3. I've seen a few ideas on Pinterest, but I feel overwhelmed about starting anything.

   4. I have no idea how to be efficient in my home!

Answer: _4_

simplified.

6. On a scale of 1-4, how much energy do you think you have wasted due to a lack of organizational systems in your home?

    1. None—my space energizes me!

    2. Some days I feel tired, but I get a boost when I get my space in order.

    3. I get exhausted just looking around my house.

    4. I'm too overwhelmed to even think about it!

Answer: 2

7. On a scale of 1-4, how would you rate the organizational systems in your home?

    1. I have great systems in place that allow me to easily restore order when life gets hectic.

    2. I have a few systems in some areas of my home, but I'd like to do more.

    3. There are hardly any systems in our home. I keep trying, but I can never seem to figure it out.

    4. Systems? What systems?

Answer: 3

Areas of Impact

8. On a scale of 1-4, when you do create an organizational system, how likely is it that you and your family will maintain it?

    1. I have some good systems that have been in place for 6+months.
    2. Every time I try to implement a system, it falls apart within a week or so.
    3. I keep buying all this stuff at The Container Store, but nothing seems to work.
    4. Systems? What systems?

Answer: _1_

9. On a scale of 1-4, how overwhelmed do you feel about organizing areas in your home?

    1. I actually get excited when I think about organizing my house!
    2. I can usually pull together a plan and make some progress.
    3. I've just stopped looking at the piles of stuff in an effort to remain calm.
    4. I get chest pain and anxiety whenever I think about trying to get started.

Answer: _2_

simplified.

10. On a scale of 1-4, how ready are you to get rid of items that are unused or don't add value to your life?

    1. Get it out! Less is better, and I'm constantly gathering up items for donation.
    2. I keep a get-rid-of bin in my closet, but I can't find time to go through my clothes.
    3. I've been saying for years that I need to start thinking about getting rid of stuff...
    4. I'm a little nervous about letting go of anything.

Answer: _1_

Your Results

Number of 1's _2_

Number of 2's _4_

Number of 3's _2_

Number of 4's _2_

Mostly 4's — You're deeply seeking organization.

Although you may have tried before to get your space organized, you're to the point now where it's easier to just avoid the clutter and chaos. You're exhausted! You often feel stressed in your home, and you see it come out when you communicate with your family. You've started to believe running a household is *supposed* to be this chaotic! A lot of time, energy and money is wasted searching for and replacing "lost" items.

There are days you find yourself going in circles trying to keep things in order, thinking to yourself, *Didn't I just pick this up?* You have clothes in your closet from ten years ago that you'd never wear, even if there was nothing else clean. You're not sure why, but you hold onto them "just in case."

The competing demands of each day and the overwhelm of just getting started keeps you feeling discouraged about organizing your home.

We have ALL felt this way at one time or another. Don't worry, there's still hope!

Mostly 2's or 3's — You're holding it together.

You're holding it together in your home, but it feels like *you're* the only one keeping it that way! This

simplified.

effort can leave you feeling frustrated...and exhausted! It makes you cringe when you think of all the time, money, and energy you waste searching for items around the house. You regularly get a wave of motivation to tidy up your closet, office or playroom, only to find yourself back in the same place a week later!

The idea of evaluating the flow of your home to create a more optimal organizational system hasn't even crossed your mind. Although your space tends to look fairly tidy most of the time, you dream about the day your family puts their own stuff away while you get some alone time, whether it's to sit and binge-watch your favorite show or simply enjoy a long walk.

You have the motivation. With a few simple steps, you can transform the chaos of your space into a calm environment.

Mostly 1's — You're an organized oasis.

Congratulations! You have a house that most people envy. Your belongings all have a home, and most of the time they get put away with only a little reminding and energy. You've invested in some organizational solutions that look great, but you find yourself working harder than you'd like to maintain them.

You often wish things could just *stay* organized. You find yourself looking at your pantry or closet thinking, *Yes, it's organized, but could it be organized better? Is there a way to organize this space that makes more sense?* A fresh perspective and more efficient systems could take you to a whole new level of calm. Be proud of yourself for taking this next step to creating a simpler and more organized space!

Relationship Clutter

Overall, my family does a pretty good job minimizing waste of time and money in our home. We keep a close eye on our spending and scheduling of activities. But I hold our living space responsible for our greatest gains and setbacks in our family harmony.

For years, my mindset to keep things in order was a constant point of contention between my me and husband. He isn't wired like me, so toys all over the floor and dishes in the sink simply don't bother him. It drove me nuts that he could just *sit* there, scrolling through his phone while I ran around trying not to pull my hair out. In my mind, picking up all the toys, clothes, and kids' crafts from all over the house was a never-ending task. I usually handled the situation by making some unkind comment to my husband, trying to make him aware that I spent my entire morning picking up with no end in sight. Not a strategy I would recommend!

I should've known our differences had a biological basis. According to UCLA's Center on Everyday Lives and Families, women react more to clutter in their homes than men do. The researchers found that women in cluttered homes have higher levels of the stress hormone cortisol. Basically, clutter triggers the alarm part of the brain, which causes a stress response, which causes a cortisol release. When clutter gets out of hand, it changes how women treat their spouse, their children, and others.[1]

I traveled to the east coast during the writing of this book to work with a client. This client, Sharon, received my services as a gift for her seventieth birthday. Sharon was ready to let go of some belongings that no longer served her. They weighed down those around her. She was motivated but didn't quite know how to go through her stuff and get rid of what she didn't want (or need) anymore. Over two days, we worked through her stuff and made great progress. She was so excited! After I arrived home, she sent me a thank you text. She said she woke up feeling "so motivated to start my day. I feel happier than I have in a long time. And more importantly, my husband seems much happier than he has in a long time."

We often don't even realize how our space is impacting us and those around us. Remember that guy in the audience with the day old dishes? He had good intentions, but he and his wife had very different reactions to the situation. I noticed how the cleanliness (or lack thereof) of our house determined how I interacted with my kids, too. If the kitchen was in disarray in the morning, I was short with my kids. Instead of sitting down, enjoying breakfast, and helping my kids start their day feeling refreshed, I ran around like a chicken on speed. I tried to set an intention for the next day. *Tomorrow, I will be a calmer, more patient wife and mother.* But I got distracted, grumpy, and downright unpleasant whenever I saw clutter. I *knew* I was anxious and agitated, so I channeled that energy into trying to create order. I felt like I couldn't sit down until the house was tidy. I wasn't even trying to get the house perfectly clean, but I just couldn't ignore the stuff lying around. It was like a little gremlin saying, "Hey, look over here!"

Luckily, I found out it wasn't just me. I met with a new client of mine in her home. "I have to admit," she said to me, "I feel vulnerable showing you the underbelly of my home." The place was beautiful in every sense. She had three kids, and their house felt like a *home* where people actually lived. As we walked through her house discussing the areas she wanted help with, I asked her what bothered her the most. "These rooms make me feel like a failure," she told me. These spaces triggered her, leading her to believe her house wasn't good enough, and therefore *she* wasn't good enough. If I didn't know what I know now, I would've thought she was silly for being so hard on herself. Instead, I understood *exactly* what was going on, and I was determined to help her. Needless to say, she's not a failure. (Think about how we show up each day if we *think* we're a failure. How do we show up for ourselves, our partners, our kids? We don't show up as the best version of ourselves.) So, we started to create systems to help her gain a new perspective on her home and herself—systems just like those you'll learn in this book.

Health Clutter

Behind my home is a beautiful open space with green grass, trees, and a pedestrian trail running through it. I'm so motivated when I see people walking and running through it every day. During the week, I have to get to the gym before my kids wake up, or it just doesn't happen. On weekends, I try to take advantage of that trail. I *try*. Many weekends, I would look at the clock first thing and think, *I'll just finish cleaning up in here and then I'll head out for a run.* In what seems like minutes later, it's late afternoon, and I'm too exhausted for a run.

Fortunately, creating good systems (like a morning routine) now allows me to follow through on my weekend morning run at 7:00 AM without stressing. I've worked with many clients who notice their simplified, systematized spaces motivate them to focus on their health goals that they used to put off.

If we want to change our beliefs, habits, or capabilities, we can start by adjusting our environment. Remember the smart part of the brain? That's where our willpower and focus "live." So, when we quiet the chaos in our environment, we "wake up" the smart part of our brain, and we're more likely to adhere to our exercise and wellness plan.

"My Kitchen Makes Me Crazy!"

I spend a lot of time helping families with their kitchens, the real heart of the home. I love how the excitement of food preparation increases once we've gotten rid of the clutter and implemented effective systems, making it that much easier to make healthy food choices.

"Yeah, I know, my messy kitchen makes me crazy!" I hear many people say. But they're not making the connection between the messy kitchen and their Oreo binges and three-quarters-of-a-bottle wine downed after the kids go to bed. No judgement here—it's all connected!

I was so excited when my client, Amy, shared how creating a system in her pantry allowed her to return to cooking and baking like she had in the past. Now that she could *see* exactly what she had in her pantry, meal planning was so much easier. She no longer got frustrated, making freezer meals or ordering take out more than she desired. She was excited to start baking again now that we had all her baking items together and easy to find. When we can see what food we actually have, we make better choices. Eating environments impact how much and what types of food we eat. Compare cluttered and uncluttered kitchen spaces. If the kitchen is a mess, you snack more. You choose unhealthy foods. In a clean kitchen, it's easier to prepare nutritious meals.

Eating aside, the greatest health impact of a simplified, organized home is reduced stress. Stress makes us experience real physiological changes—from high blood pressure and elevated heart rates, to migraines or worse. Rarely are we aware that our physical space contributes so much to our health. Now that I'm not spending all my time cleaning up "just one more thing," I have more time to focus on *me*. I now have a special place in our home where I spend at least three mornings a week doing my Miracle Morning routine—meditating, journaling, and reading. When I start my mornings this way, my days are *so* much better. I feel more centered, productive and optimistic. When I take care of my own needs, I show up as a better mom, wife, and ultimately, a better version of myself—and that's the greatest gift I can offer. (To learn more about the Miracle Morning, check out *The Miracle Morning for Parents and Families* by Mike and Lindsay McCarthy.)

Money Clutter

If you want fit finances, the first step is a lean environment! Imagine the average person who has a little too much stuff cluttering their home. Someone who needs help creating systems that make their home lives easier. My client, Michelle, fit that description. She made a New Year's resolution to go through and simplify each room in her house. Michelle started her simplifying journey in her closet. It drove her crazy every time she opened it. She could never find anything to wear even though it was packed from floor to ceiling with beautiful clothes.

As we worked our way through her closet, she found piles of clothes she'd never worn, tags still attached. Once we'd gone through all her clothes, she had found over $1,000 worth of unused items to return to various stores! In her newly organized closet, which she now calls her "oasis," Michelle can get dressed in five minutes, leaving her more time to spend with her children before work and school—even time for a morning workout class! Aside from the time savings, she simply felt more motivated. I love seeing results of clearing a space that we never anticipated! Now she actually *enjoys* being in her closet.

Michelle's case might be extreme, but it illustrates how much money we can waste buying things that just sit around unused. Another benefit Michelle shared with me after cleaning out her closet is how much faster she packs now when she travels. This is very valuable to her, as she was traveling back and forth a lot to care for her ill mother. To remove even one source of stress from this situation is meaningful. Without messy closets or cluttered spaces to distract her, she has a few more moments to kiss her kids goodbye before heading off to the airport.

After we'd worked our way through Michelle's closet, we focused on the source of her clutter (shopping) to avoid ending up right back where we'd started. She's now being more intentional with her buying habits. She hasn't stopped shopping completely, but she's made a significant decrease in her purchases. She's now a more mindful consumer. The $1,000 find, the extra time with her kids, and the stress decrease while traveling might make it seem like Michelle just got lucky. But she was *fortunate*, not lucky. Luck implies her discovery was accidental. I can certainly tell you, it wasn't!

Another client took my online masterclass *Simplify Your Space, Simplify Your Life*. She was nervous about her first assignment to simplify a small space. But once she'd started, all the little "treasures" she unearthed made it exciting! If I had a dollar for every time I heard, "Oh my goodness! I've been looking everywhere for this!" I'd be at the beach with a cabana bartender serving me umbrella drinks!

I sometimes joke with my clients that the fine print in my contract states I get a percentage of any money or gift cards they find while we're cleaning. It happens *all* the time. No lie! One client found almost *$8,000* in uncashed paychecks. How anyone cannot miss that kind of money is a mystery to me. But when our space is *that* crazy, we become *that* forgetful. What might be hiding in *your* cluttered drawers?

Another client of mine *loves* to collect free promotional items at various events. My husband does this, too. After working with me, she started to see her affection for these trinkets dwindle. She realized that they just end up in her junk drawer, creating more work for her down the road. Now she texts me when she's at an event, "You would be so proud of me! I didn't get anything!" with a picture of a promotional table. I love it!

I believe the universe sends you little rewards for clearing out your space. Once you begin, your motivation to *keep* it clear increases. If you found out you had a dairy allergy and removed dairy from your diet, you'd know how good it feels to be off of it. You wouldn't even *want* to go back to it, no matter how good that ice cream tastes. And once you've cleaned out your spaces, you won't *want* to purchase that new pair of shoes you don't need. You'll also realize just how much stuff you already have. Once you have systems in place to help you manage your home with less stress, you'll buy less because you become more efficient and resourceful. You re-purchase less because you can actually find things now!

When I was helping my sister-in-law, we found so much stuff she thought she had "lost." We found a $70 medication for her dog that she'd just had to repurchase, a large bottle of ibuprofen that she had repurchased, *and* a large stash of batteries that she had, you guessed it, repurchased. She found a "lost" gift card to Costco, as well as clothes she'd been looking for. It was like Christmas!

I have a client, Lisa, who enlisted my services to prepare for an upcoming home sale and out of state move. She couldn't take her belongings with her when she moved initially, so I helped get her things into a storage unit. I also helped her work with movers when time came to move to her new home. She *still* couldn't take everything, so some stayed in storage. This illustrates another way our stuff costs us when we have to pay for storage and transport. Things that cost us so much and add such little value hardly seem worth the effort!

Let's follow the journey of just *one* item in Lisa's storage unit. Lisa had a storage bin of very nice stationery she purchased on sale several years ago. Let's say she got it at fifty percent off and paid ten bucks. It sat in her basement for a few years. Not much added cost there. Not much added value either! But then she paid me to help her sort and pack it. She paid movers to move it to the storage unit. She decided *not* to move it to her new place, so now she's paying to store it. The storage unit is around $300 per month. Eventually she'll make a trip back to sort through her remaining items in the unit. Factor in the cost of that trip, the cost of my services to help her again, and any costs to haul away any unwanted items. Even if she was to sell the set of stationary for the ten dollars that she originally paid for it (which is very unlikely) she'd *still* be *losing* money based on what she paid to sort, move, and store it. Ultimately, this stationary may have brought her joy when she purchased it, but ended up costing $3600 a year to keep! To make matters worse, on top of moving, starting a new job, and relocating to a new city, she divorced her spouse. Too often I see people dealing with divorce, death, or other major life events while they're trying to sort through all of their stuff. Is it really worth it?

I admit, I used to be a "bargain" shopper. I used to search all the clearance racks just to get a "good deal." I'd find a new shirt for four dollars or a great pair of jeans for under twenty. Even though I found a lot of new favorites, I also purchased a bunch of crap because of the discounts. As a result, many of them went unworn and ended up in the donation pile months later. I was really *losing* money, not saving it. I know I'm not alone—I've seen many closets with lots of tags still hanging on clothes with the discounted price written in the ever-famous red pen.

Aside from the wasted money, there's the ethical factor of purchasing deeply discounted, easily disposable items with manufacturing conditions that allow these clothes to be sold at such low prices. If you're ever interested in knowing where your "bargain" clothes come from and the impact they have on our environment, check out the documentary *The True Cost*. They state on their website:

> The True Cost is a story about clothing. It's about the clothes we wear, the people who make them, and the impact the industry is having on our world. The price of clothing has been decreasing for decades, while the human and environmental costs have grown dramatically. The True Cost is a groundbreaking documentary film that pulls back the curtain on the untold story and asks us to consider, who really pays the price for our clothing?

> ...an unprecedented project that invites us on an eye opening journey around the world and into the lives of the many people and places behind our clothes.[2]

This film moved me even further to become a more mindful consumer. When you start seeing the effects of less clutter in your own spaces, I bet you'll become a more mindful consumer, too.

Time Clutter

The time I saved after simplifying our house and creating effective systems for the spaces we used most was *astounding*. From sunrise to sunset, I've experienced the benefits of simplification. From the simple system that helps me be more efficient with making my kids' lunch, I save five minutes every morning, which, over the course of a year, is 950 lunches and twenty-two hours saved. This is just one small system—I have other systems all over our house!

I get excited for my clients when they tell me they now have more time for the important things. That's what it's really about. It's not about the space, but what the space *does* for us. It's about how we focus on what's truly meaningful for us versus wasting our time and energy on mundane tasks. It's about getting in that class at the gym instead of picking up clothes from the floor. It's about taking time to sit and relax instead of running around getting everyone else ready. The average person spends forty minutes a day looking for items such as phone, wallet, and keys (Cue Adam Sandler's song *Phone Wallet Keys*). What could you do with an extra forty minutes per day? That's almost five hours per week! Maybe catching up on your favorite show? Finishing that novel you started? Picking up a new hobby as a family? Learning a new exercise or sport?

My husband used to misplace his keys and wallet constantly, always running back into the house in the morning before leaving for work. We'd all ransack the house to help him. I even bought him those little tracking devices to help him find his belongings, but the batteries died. Insert the music that plays in Pac-Man when you're on your last life and get eaten by a ghost! Instead of relying on another device, we created a system and worked to develop a habit where he would hang his keys every night when he would come in. It took some training, and he still misplaces things, but it's made his morning, and those around him, easier.

simplified.

Simple systems can help everyone, no matter how we're wired. No matter how different we are from our spouses or our children, we can ALL stop wasting time every day. Systems make your daily "chores" take less time, freeing you up to partake in activities you enjoy, but usually avoid because you're too tired (refer back to the illustration of the energy bank in Chapter 2). When you clear your space, life is more meaningful.

Summary:

- Clutter impacts many aspects of our lives.
    - Relationships: We communicate less effectively when our space is out of order. It also causes a strain in relationships as we are all wired differently.
    - Health: We have more time to take care of ourselves and feel more motivated when our space is clear and includes systems.
    - Money: We repurchase less when we can find our belongings and we become more mindful consumers when we clear our space.
    - Time: We spend less time searching for items when we can easily find them. We move through our spaces and daily tasks when our spaces our less cluttered.

CHAPTER 4

Simple Isn't Always Easy

Michelle went looking for organization in her closet, and she found time *and* money. Clearing out her closet was a great accomplishment, but things in her house didn't change overnight. It's hard to break habits in adults. One day I went to her house, and in her entryway sat a pile of newly delivered boxes from Target and Amazon.

"What are all the boxes?" I asked.

A guilty look passed over her face. "Well, they aren't all for me," she mumbled.

"Mom, what about all the hard work you've done with Stephanie? Isn't it wasted if you keep bringing new stuff into the house?" her twelve-year-old daughter asked her.

From the mouths of babes. Lasting change occurs in small steps, and Michelle *was* making progress in reducing her overall shopping. People who change habits cold turkey often relapse. Let's look at what goes into making those changes.

Barriers to Change

By now, it's not news to you that simplified environments are more calming than cluttered ones. So, if we *know* we feel better when our spaces are clear, why isn't everything organized and simplified already? Why do we still have spaces that are cluttered? What are the barriers to getting our spaces in order?

Some of my clients have the motivation to get rid of stuff, but lack the follow through. Cluttered spaces overwhelm us. Overwhelm leads to procrastination. And most people don't know where to start. They make excuses. They feel defeated. They feel like crying just thinking about it. The guilt and fear sets in before the work even begins. When we're in these spaces, we function from the alarm part of our brain.

The number one reason people call me is that they need someone to help them move through the overwhelm stage. When I go through items with my clients to suggest parting with them, they often say, "I'm afraid..." The sentence ends with, "I may need it someday," or, "I might hurt so-and-so's feelings." Fear holds people back. I guide them through these hurdles, helping them see that if the day comes they actually *need* three garlic presses or fourteen legal notepads, they likely won't be able to find them.

A big hurdle in letting go of things is *guilt*. If you're worried your friend may find out that you got rid of the creepy collector doll that your kid's afraid of, she'll *never* know. "I feel bad, Aunt Milly gave me this china set." She gave it to you thirty-five years ago. You've never taken it out of the box. Several pieces are probably missing. You'll probably *never use it,* and Aunt Milly will *never* know! I tell my clients they don't want to put their children in the position of having to decide what to do with *your* junk. Stop the cycle and stop delaying the inevitable. If it doesn't add value to your life and you wouldn't put it on display in your house? Let. It. Go.

When we receive gifts from family or friends that we have no use for and, quite frankly, don't even *like*, we feel bad when we get rid of them. This is why I've stopped gifting people "things" and started giving gift

simplified.

certificates or experiences that they'll enjoy instead. I don't want to be creating guilt for anyone.

Regardless of what's holding someone back from letting go of stuff, deep down, they know they want to get rid of it. They just need someone to help them make that final decision. I had a client recently who said that the greatest benefit of working with me was the "psychological aspect". It's as though I gave her "permission" to let things go. I always tell my clients I'll meet them where they're at. I don't come with a one-size-fits-all approach. I help them set their goals, determine their starting point, and keep them on track. Just like working with heart patients in the past, they all start from a different place with different limitations. I'm not going to make everyone run a five kilometer race. That's not realistic! But you *can* get started.

Getting Started

Most people try to purge their entire homes all at once instead of breaking the work down into smaller chunks. They have no clear, structured plan or process. Stressed and frazzled, they start with the biggest, most overwhelming projects, such as basements or garages. Then they're at their breaking point. They say, "I can't take it anymore! I'm throwing everything out!" But they stop before they even start. Large areas are neither quick nor easy. I usually suggest starting with a small space to *practice* sorting through things, then moving things to their proper home. Starting with a small space, such as a junk drawer or small closet, builds your confidence. You get excited from the accomplishment. Our brains like that sense of accomplishment, and you'll gain more momentum that way.

Most people underestimate how long it takes to go through a space. That's another reason it's best to start small. If you need to contemplate every item's future in your life, the work takes a while. I suggest enlisting the support of a professional or a good friend to keep you on track, especially with your first decluttering project. Preferably not a family member. We love them, but they can be impatient, opinionated, and make deciding what to do with that baby blanket even more emotional. Remember Sharon? She received my services for her 70th birthday? Before enlisting my help, her family tried to assist her going through her spaces. It didn't go so well. The ironic thing is, I was saying the same things to her as her family members had. For some reason, when it came from a third party, she listened. Too often we have emotions tied to messages when they come from loved ones.

simplified.

Clutter vs. Hoarding

By now, you're probably thinking about all the spaces in your house you want to tackle, and you might be fearing the word "hoarder." Honestly, you're probably *not* in as bad a shape as you think you are. They have the average American household accumulation of stuff—too many clothes, unused home decor, and outgrown kids' items. They're motivated to make life easier, and they just need a spotter to keep them from falling.

So don't worry—you're probably not a "hoarder"! According to the American Psychiatric Association, hoarding is a disorder with a clinical diagnosis.[1] Hoarding symptoms include:

1. Lasting problems with throwing out or giving away possessions, regardless of actual value.

2. A perceived need to save the items and distress when parting with them.

3. Items filling, blocking, and cluttering active living spaces so they cannot be used easily or at all.

Some of you may feel that number one and two describe you, but in my mind, number three separates people with clutter issues from those who fit the hoarding diagnosis. When your stuff is impacting your ability to live in your space, it's a more serious situation. I've heard so many people over the years claim they're hoarders. They're not. Quite frankly, it's hard *not* to feel like a hoarder with the amount of stuff that comes into our lives every day. I don't work with extreme hoarders, as I don't believe my skill set supports them appropriately. (If all three of these criteria apply to you, it's okay! There *are* professionals who can help. A great first step is scheduling an appointment with a local therapist who can help you come up with a plan to address your hoarding.)

Most individuals I work with have the motivation, but they just don't make lasting progress because they apply "technical solutions" to "adaptive challenges." In my healthcare leadership development days, I studied and taught the theories of leadership expert Ronald Heifetz. Heifetz's understanding of technical solutions plays a role in the work I do today in my clients' homes. In a chaotic or cluttered home, a technical solution would be to label everything, shove it into bins, and call it a day. A week later, you're right back where you started. It's like weight loss. You go on crazy diets, lose a bunch of weight, but then gain it back (and then some) a month later.

I want my clients to dig deeper, to get to the root of their chaos or clutter, and stop the cycle where it begins. In these situations, *technical* solutions aren't helpful because you're dealing with an *adaptive* challenge. Addressing the adaptive challenge requires that you find out what got you here in the first place. Are you bringing too much stuff into the house? Do you lack systems to maintain the space? Both? When you focus on your behaviors and habits, you can identify what systems might work best. Yes, bins can be fun to buy and label, but they won't solve your problems unless they're part of a bigger system.

I've had so many people contact me for help after they've spent hundreds of dollars at The Container Store on bins, shelves, and other organizational gadgets, only to find themselves even more discouraged a week later. Unless you simplify and create systems, these gadgets won't save you time or money. And they'll only further strain your relationships because you'll bark at everyone for not using the bins the way you ask them to!

I met with a mom who had tried her best to organize her entry way. She had coat and outdoor gear bins for each kid, all clearly labeled. They refused to use them. Or so she thought. When I took a look in the bins, I saw an abyss of gloves, hats, and other random items, like a goodie bag from a birthday party. The bins were so full, her boys couldn't fit anything else into them.

That was the reason they weren't using them. They had too much stuff for that system to be effective!

After going through the items in the entryway—donating what they no longer needed and finding new homes for things that didn't need to be in the entryway—we evaluated how things were set up. We then arranged things based on how her boys used them. As a result, it was much easier for them to grab and return their outdoor gear—and *only* their outdoor gear—to those bins. Happy mom, happy everyone!

That's what I want for you. What worked for her entryway can work for any space in your home. All it takes is some simplifying, systematizing, and sustaining. Grab my "Entryway Guide" for more ideas at www.lifemadesimpleathome.com/resources.

Three Steps to Less Stress in Your Space

Many women I have worked with express that they feel like they have "lost control" in their homes and lives. Most often when you say you want to get "organized", you mean that you want to regain control of your environment and life. That's what I wanted in my home, and what most of my clients are searching for when they ask for my help. We don't need things to be perfect, but we want some sense of control in our homes and lives—a sense of sanity.

I wanted to create a process to approach my home that was realistic. One that created a sense of sanity and control. The process I've outlined in this book has helped many of my clients to be successful in achieving that sanity. This same three-step process I take every client through turns chaos and clutter into calm and sanity. Those three steps are *simplify, systematize,* and *sustain.* Let me show you how it's done.

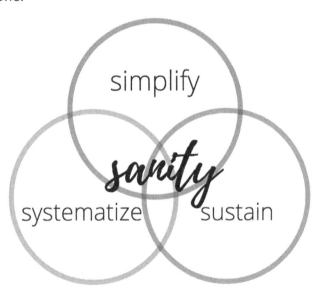

Summary:

- Letting go of stuff is not easy. Common barriers are overwhelm, guilt, and fear.

- Starting small can help to reduce the overwhelm and gain some momentum clearing your space.

- Simplify, systematize, and sustain—these three steps will help you clear your space and gain back your energy.

CHAPTER 5

Simplify

The Simplest, Hardest Thing

"The hardest thing in the world is to simplify your life. It's so easy to make it complex."[1]

Yvon Chouinard, billionaire rock climber turned environmentalist, and founder of Patagonia, is right.

In the life simplification industry, it's widely known that each of us (on average) only use twenty percent of our belongings on a regular basis. That means eighty percent of our stuff is just taking up valuable space—in our closets and minds. Do the math on that, and you're paying a mortgage or leasing an apartment for not even *one-quarter* of your space. Quit ripping yourself off!

simplified.

That's why my first step is simplify. We have way more than we need. And if we're only using twenty percent of it, then it's safe to say the other eighty percent is not adding value. When people think about letting stuff go, they mostly focus on what they're giving up—not what they're getting in return. You can't put it off forever. The stuff will not miraculously pare itself down. In reality, it will only continue to get worse if you do not take some type of action. Once you start to experience the benefits of simplifying, you will get *excited* about letting go of more. I promise.

If it's your closet that seems overwhelming, take a breath and get a sense of what's inside. Determine what *needs* to be there, and what's just wasting space. Weed out clothing that no longer fits, that isn't comfortable, or that you simply never wear. Pare down to only what you need, and you'll make space for other more important things in your life. This applies to *all* aspects of your life.

Having too much stuff in one area of our life inevitably runs over into other aspects of our life. One day I was meeting with a client and she was feeling very emotional about life in general. I totally understand how the demands and responsibilities of running a household can bring you to tears sometimes. We were discussing the different aspects that felt overwhelming and she actually made the connection between her overflowing closet and her overflowing laundry basket. This was also a point of contention between her and her husband- the laundry responsibilities.

When we simplified the wardrobe, we also simplified her laundry process alleviating a lot of stress and unnecessary work in her home. Again, the less we have the less we have to manage and the less strain it puts on our relationships.

Whether it's your closet or your calendar, start with the "low-hanging fruit" (meaning the easiest to pick!). Getting rid of eighty percent of your wardrobe seems daunting and unrealistic to most people, so I suggest starting small. The easiest, simplest way to start letting go is to ask yourself honestly, "Does this even serve a purpose in my life?"

If you use it often, if it makes your life easier, it's adding value. Stuff that does *not* add value is your collection of trophies from your high school tennis career that sit in a box gathering dust in the basement. If they brought you joy, they wouldn't be in that box—they'd be on display. But that might be weird.

simplified.

Simplifying Can Be Simple

Let me share my best tips to simplify, *simply*.

Inventory your stuff. Pull everything out. This may seem daunting, especially when you're already overwhelmed, but it's a very important part of the simplifying process. When we pull everything out of a space, whether it's a drawer or an entire garage (reminder—your garage is *not* the best place to start, especially if you're a rookie!) it serves multiple purposes. It requires that we see and touch everything that is in the space. I often see my clients try to get away with scanning a space visually, but we just can't get a true sense of what's actually there if we don't physically pick things up. We're less effective at paring down, and we miss finding those hidden treasures we thought were lost! It gives us a fresh perspective on the space. This is very helpful when we're implementing a new system.

Organize items as you pull them out. As you pull each item out, decide what category it fits into, so you can create a space for each category when you're finished. Start with these three basic categories: **Keep** (it adds value to your life, or you use it regularly.) **Go** (you're done with it, so donate it, give it away, recycle it, or throw it in the trash). **Not sure** (if you're struggling with something, create this category, but know you'll have to go through it again! Don't use this as a crutch to keep things you don't need, but more as a tool to keep you moving forward and not getting stuck on one item). Notice there is not a "just in case pile".

Organize your "keep" pile. This will vary depending on the area. Put similar items together to help you in your systems creation and implementation. For example, organize items in your pantry into baking, sauces, grains, cereals, snacks, etc. If you're like most of my clients, this is where you'll discover four jars of baking powder that you're not likely to use before they expire—oh wait, two of them are *already* expired! You can also organize your keep pile by determining things you are keeping but need a new home in the house— for example, winter gloves that keep landing on the desk. (More on systems and how to prevent this from happening later.)

When you start to simplify, it doesn't have to be a massive overhaul of letting go of everything all at once. It's okay if it takes a few attempts! I see this as a journey. Sometimes you have to start small. Realize that you *will* survive, even if you let go of the Banana Republic sweater you got on sale in 2008 and never actually wore.

On the first pass, I usually see people get rid of ten to twenty percent of the items in their first area. Once we go to put things away, they tend to realize there's even more they don't need. Then they start to gain some momentum for letting go of other items. I encourage them to ride this momentum. People start feeling so much lighter! As long as you're working towards paring down to items that add value and bring joy, you'll end up with an smaller amount of stuff that makes it possible to implement an effective system.

My client Michelle has continued to get rid of clothes in her closet. Every time we meet she tells me, "I want to get rid of more!" She sees and feels the benefits of simplifying. So many of her clothes go unworn! She told me one of her new criteria for keeping an article of clothing is if someone compliments her on it. I love the idea of only keeping clothes that make you feel good when you wear them! Who *doesn't* feel good when someone tells you they like your outfit?

Sentimental Objects

This chapter wouldn't be complete without discussing sentimental objects. Now, this is *not* where you want to start when paring down your belongings. But if you're committed to simplifying, you will need to tackle these more difficult items eventually.

Even though I'm not a very sentimental person, I understand these things aren't easy to get rid of. The fact is, objects don't carry memories. We don't store memories in a box in our basement. The memory is not lost if we let the item go. If the item means that much to you, it should be on display.

Some people I've worked with are ready to let go of things that have sentimental value, but they need help. They need a *strategy*. I like to start by setting parameters. Find a nice box and let that be your guide. You can only keep what fits in that box. Remember grandma's hope chest? She only kept what fit inside. Yet her memories and stories lasted a lifetime. Less stuff, more memories. A powerful lesson.

Kids' Toys

Kids' toys is the other topic that I am asked about A LOT. If I could wave a wand and make the challenge of managing kids' toys vanish, I would retire early and enjoy my days in a mountain house. But seriously, as a mom of two kids, I understand this issue firsthand. I used to find myself going in circles trying to keep up with my kids' pace of taking toys out and laying them all over the floor! I have tried a variety of ways to organize them - by color, age, theme, etc. I seemed to

simplified.

get the same result until I really started to simplify. I don't think there is a secret solution, but letting go of perfection and actually letting go of the toys has been key for me to stop my cycle of insanity. Less is so much more with kiddos! Just a few interesting findings about kids and toys:

- British research found that the average ten-year-old owns 238 toys but plays with just twelve daily.[2]
- 3.1% of the world's children live in America, but they own 40% of the toys consumed globally.[3]

In my opinion, our kids do not need as many toys as we allow them to have. We actually overwhelm them and trigger their brains negatively with too many options. The fewer toys they have, the more creative they can be. Before even trying to implement some kind of system, let's reduce the number of toys we have to manage!

Simply pare them down and donate some of the toys. Depending on your children's ages and willingness to let go of things, you could do this with them...or without them. Many people say that the kiddos should be a part of this activity. I think it all depends on how they will accept it.

I ask my younger kids to pick one toy they no longer use and would like to give to a kid who is in need. Then I go through and pick out the ones they have outgrown or haven't used in a long time and are not likely to miss. I also go through their stuff when they are at school, and I toss all of the little pieces and broken items that will never get fixed or paired back up. Let them go! When I find little pieces I have picked up a few times off the floor, they have a new home—in the trash bin. I have become very creative about hiding these items in the trash. Some people may think this is extreme or wasteful. I agree it's wasteful, and I do feel guilty sometimes. This is why I try not to bring more than we actually need into our house. I do not want to be contributing to the trash problem so I try to be intentional about what I or others give to my kids.

If there are a good number of toys your kids still play with and are not ready to let go, I suggest taking a handful of toys and tucking them away. You can pull these out when they seem to be getting bored with the current toys. This could also be a strategy for letting go of some toys. You can tuck some away and if they don't notice after several months, it may be an opportunity to donate them.

simplified.

To learn more about creating a system for kids' toys, grab your free Kids' Toys Guide at www.lifemadesimpleathome.com/resources

Summary:

- Most of us only use twenty percent of our belongings, meaning the other eighty percent are just taking up space

- When you simplify, start with the easy stuff or start with a small space.

- Go through each item in the space and break into categories: Keep, Go, Not Sure (use this last category sparingly, and be sure to go back through it after your first pass).

- Tackle sentimental items last or at least wait until you have gained some momentum and confidence. Instead of storing a large number of these items in your basement never to be seen, pick a few to put on display or find a reasonably sized box to store the most meaningful ones.

- Kids only need so many toys. The more they have the more there is to pick up. Limiting their toys is easier and more enjoyable for all.

CHAPTER 6

Systematize

The Magic of a System

Creating a system is my favorite step in the whole three-step process. This is where the real magic happens! Remember my professional training and experience in healthcare creating systems for procedures? That's exactly what you're going to do in your home. Your systems will maximize efficiency, add value to your life by saving you time, money, and energy, and conserve your brain power for the important things.

In healthcare, systems have saved billions of dollars, hundreds of thousands of lives, and improved the quality of care patients receive in immeasurable ways.

Although we can't claim these impressive numbers in our homes, we can still make quite a significant impact on a smaller scale. Isn't your sanity worth a lot of money? What about the special moments with your family that we can easily miss? Priceless.

But if we're talking dollars and cents, you often *can* measure your savings directly. When we have efficient systems in our homes and our lives, we save money in so many ways—like re-purchasing items we can't find, buying something we forgot we already had, or paying fees for forgetting or misplacing a bill! Systems also make us feel more in control, and we tend to make fewer frivolous purchases due to stress or boredom.

Creating systems in a work environment is often easier than it is at home. People already put their best foot forward at work. At home, we tend to relax into our bad habits. We don't have the motivation of formal evaluations with potential bonuses when we follow a system at home. But as you'll see, the rewards can be even *more* fulfilling.

I should mention that my own house isn't immaculate by any means. But having less stuff and knowing everything has a home means I can quickly restore order when things get nutty. The very important result of creating a system and maintaining your sanity is that all the items you own need to have a home. Piles (and frustration) develop when we do not have proper homes for things.

I'm constantly looking at spaces in our home to figure out how we can create more effective systems. I love coming up with ideas for our garage, kitchen, or playroom, and my husband usually just bites his tongue. I'm so grateful I have hundreds of clients' homes to have this kind of fun in. Otherwise, I might drive my husband crazy!

Once you've simplified a space and pared down your items, it's time to create a system—which is really more a verb than a noun. I define systematizing as creating a process that makes the space more efficient, easier to use, and works *with* the flow of your home, rather than *against* it. A system can be as simple as how, where, or when you do a particular activity or place something.

Real Systems (In the Real World)

How does a system look in the real world? I organized Michelle's clothing space based on how and when she wore which clothes, making sure she could get ready easily and efficiently every day. Before we worked together she had some clothes in the closet and others

simplified.

out in her bedroom dresser. She was going back and forth getting dressed and often getting sidetracked in the process. We moved all the clothes related to her work, this included undergarments, to her closet so she could just go in there after her shower and get completely dressed. I also factored in her thought process when she goes to go look for a particular item. If she is looking for a blouse, will she look for it by style, color or sleeve length. This helped me to arrange things most effectively for her.

This isn't as complicated as it might seem. Start by mapping the process you already follow in your space. What steps do you take to perform a particular activity, like getting ready in the morning? Does the space work with your natural behaviors, habits, and rhythm? What's the journey of an item to reach its final destination? How many times do you touch or move an item to get it where it belongs?

Take an example outside of your bedroom. Look at the steps you follow to clean your kitchen. When I wanted a better system for storing dishes, I started storing them in the cabinets nearest the dishwasher. Now when it's time to unload the dishwasher, I can stand in one place and put almost all the dishes away, instead of walking back and forth across the kitchen. Just like the surgical techs and nurses in the procedure room, I reduced the amount of time it took me to perform the task. Five minutes might not seem like a spectacular savings, but when you do dishes every day (and it's one of your least favorite things to do!) you want it to be as fast and as easy as possible. That savings adds up to thirty minutes a week, or twenty-six hours a year!

I'm not suggesting you write down *every* step you take in your kitchen on a notepad, but if you simply pause to become *aware* of them—cabinet to kitchen island, island to fridge, back to island, to drawer, to cabinet, back to island again, to fridge, and then all over again—you'll surprise yourself. You'll realize just how inefficient you are. Creating a simple system that only requires you to go from fridge to cabinet to kitchen island cuts out the steps you really don't need. Fewer steps means more time and energy.

Another area most likely to lack a good system is our entryway, making our departures each morning more hectic than they need to be. What does your process look like here? When you walk through your door each day after work, what's in your hands? Where does your stuff land? When you head out each morning, how many times do you run back and forth from the kitchen to the bedroom to the entryway and back searching for

simplified.

things? Remember my dear husband's morning dilemma? Entryways are a great opportunity to create your first system, one that allows things to reach their proper home easily, while avoiding piles on the floor or countertops.

Creating Your Zones

Closet, kitchen, entryway—each of these areas is a "zone." Zones are high-activity areas we use frequently with a particular purpose. Mapping out your zones can save you a lot of time. For example, in the kitchen, we pack lunches, cook, store food, wash dishes, and (most importantly, in my house!) make coffee.

We're more efficient with these daily activities if we have designated spaces and systems with which to perform them. To systematize your kitchen zone, identify an area of the kitchen that makes the most sense for *each specific* activity. Obviously, cooking needs to happen at the stove, and dishwashing at the sink. But what about lunch prep? Think about where it makes the most sense for you. If you have everything you need for lunch prep stored closely together—lunch boxes, containers, snacks, etc.—you can save a significant amount of time.

Systematizing isn't always easy. Too often, we're blinded into seeing a space the way we've *always* seen it. Plates and bowls get stored in two different cabinets on opposite sides of the kitchen because, well, that's where they've always been! Pulling everything out of the space allows you to see the space with fresh eyes. You'll discover new ways to use the space, and you'll be able to step back and think about what *really* happens in that zone. Then, as you find new homes for items that were in that space, you can intentionally reserve that space for the items associated with that zone's activities.

Now, everyone's kitchen is laid out differently. Some are small, some are large. I had a client in my online masterclass who said she couldn't create systems because her kitchen was too small. I disagree. A system can be created within a single shelf, cupboard, or drawer. It's about giving things a home that works with the flow of your space, and making a particular activity in that space easier. To grab a complete guide to creating systems in your kitchen, visit www.lifemadesimpleathome.com/resources.

Frequency of Use

I encourage my clients to leverage storage spaces that are easy to reach (your "prime real estate") for items you and your family use regularly. Keep less frequently used items in an area that's out of the way or up high. For example, serving platters that are just used for entertaining should be placed on the top shelf and not down low where your daily dishes should go. This makes returning frequently used items to their designated home much easier, and they're more likely to be there the next time you go look for them! Compare taking the extra second to put something back in its designated space to the ease of tossing it onto the nearest countertop. You'll be glad you took the time to put it in its right place. Next time, it'll take a few seconds to find it, rather than half an hour hunting through the house.

Find Your Flow

At this point, you might be motivated to toss this book onto *your* kitchen island and get to work. In a spur-of-the-moment decision, I've watched some clients "organize" a zone or put things back after the Simplify step without actually looking at what happens in that space. In the entryway, they design a system for where shoes and backpacks *should* land, where papers *should* pile up, and where keys *should* go, but not factoring in where they actually *do* land.

Systematize

When you're trying to find a proper home for your items, think about your flow. What is actually happening in the space. What makes sense for *you* and *your* family's lifestyle? Where do things typically land? Where would you first think to look for something? What would you associate it with?

Finding proper homes for each item (and making it easy to return them to that home) prevents piles and frustration. This is especially important if you're creating a system that an entire household needs to use. In a space like your entryway, you'll need to factor in all the above questions for them as well. What might make sense for your kids when creating a system for their shoes? What might makes sense for your spouse or roommate when creating a system for keys and bags?

For example, if your kiddos come in the back door after school and the bags are landing by the door, when trying to create a home for them, avoid putting hooks for the bags by the front door as this is does not flow with the traffic and behaviors in your home. Instead, find a spot where they can hang them near where they are landing now. This will make it simple and there is a greater chance they will adhere.

simplified.

Sometimes creating systems requires more than fifteen minutes of effort. It often take a few tries to get the system right, as we often *think* we know what happens in a space. Reality frequently surprises us. Isn't it worth the difference between your sanity and your house returning to a hot mess in a week? We need to dig deep to figure out what works best for you in your home. I love when I'm working with a client, and they look at me with amazement and say, "I never thought about it that way!"

Instead of brainstorming the perfect system and trying to force your family to follow it, <u>build your system around behaviors and habits that already exist</u>. Good intentions alone will never beat bad habits. How can we shift our habits so we work *with* them instead of *against* them? If we want to create change in our home and our life, we need to think about what new habits we can create as well. When you're looking at a space trying to determine the best system to implement, factor in the motivation of everyone who regularly uses the space. Most people *can* keep a space tidy, but they simply aren't *motivated* to do so. If your spouse and kids aren't motivated to put their shoes away, then you'd better have a foolproof, easy-to-follow system for shoe storage—or good bribes! Build your system *around* existing behaviors, like the backpacks at the back door, and keep the least motivated people in mind.

My husband is oblivious to dirty clothes on the floor and the explosion of the kids' toys across the kitchen. For years, his shoes landed in the middle of our mudroom. I tried every tactic I could think of (short of a shock collar) to get him to take his shoes off at the door. After many conversations (or on my end, complaining sessions), I *finally* got him to agree to take them off by the door. But by some dark force, they wound up in the middle of the room once again. I put a shoe organizer on the back of the door. I thought this was perfect! It looked good, and it was so simple. Cleary, he didn't notice it. The shoes continued to land in the middle of the room.

So, did I cave? Did I give up? Well...not exactly. I got smarter. I built my system *around* his habit instead of trying to change it. I placed a shoe tray where his shoes were landing. After his shoes landed, I pushed the tray under our bench. Out of sight, out of mind!

As you can see, the worst system for a family is one that only *you* want to use! I'm not trying to be critical of my husband, or give up on keeping our house in order. Habits are stored in a very efficient part of our brain. This is why we can do something repeatedly, day in and day out, without even thinking about it. This is also why it's hard to change the behavior of a forty-year-old man.

Kids are much easier to create new habits with because their current habits aren't hard-wired yet like adults' are. For them, simple systems work well. The easier a system is to follow, the more motivated they'll feel to follow it. As we teach our kids new, positive behaviors and implement new habits, positive reinforcement is always effective and helpful. When it comes to adults, we need to remember to be patient, as hard as it may be. Some habits may have been formed over twenty or thirty years, so they're not going to change overnight! The next time you find yourself wishing your spouse would just pick up their stuff, remind yourself that they're only human with a wired brain.

Make a system simple to use repeatedly, and you're on your way to creating a new, positive habit. It also helps if you make it *really* hard to return to the old habit. If your kids are used to throwing papers on the table, move the table or put something else on it while you're trying to implement the new habit.

Summary:

- A system is where, when, or how you do something, saving you time and energy.

- Create zones in highly utilized spaces and create systems within each of these spaces.

- Factor in behaviors and habits of others who utilize these spaces when creating systems. You'll avoid frustration and increase the chance of the space functioning as you intend.

- Systems are easier to change than behaviors, so keep things simple if you want others to follow.

CHAPTER 7

Sustain

Creating a clear, calm environment is a journey. It's not a one-and-done event you accomplish in a day. Just like my overall process has three steps (Simplify, Systems, Sustain), the Sustain step contains three actions: be intentional about consuming less, purge regularly, and maintain your systems.

I teach these to all of my clients. Michelle could have stopped after we recouped a thousand bucks from her closet. But after we tackled the remaining rooms of her house, we focused on how she could sustain her clutter-free home going forward. What happens when I walk out the door, and my clients are left to face their daily life alone? The Sustain step involves identifying what's at the core of your issue.

simplified.

Bringing Stuff Back In

Create your own filter that aligns with your goals for your home—and stick to it. Be stubborn about it! When you're deciding what to bring into your home, run the decision through your filter: "Will this item align with my goals and intentions? Do I *really* need this? Will this be one more thing in a pile on my counter?"

It can be a difficult question, especially when it comes to free stuff. Because my husband and I had our kids later in life, we were fortunate enough to receive hand-me-downs from our friends with older kids. We got stuck in the habit of saying, "Yes!" whenever someone offered us free baby stuff. We had to start catching ourselves. When we decided to go down the path of living with less stuff, we realized that also meant less *free* stuff. Stuff for the sake of stuff no longer aligned with our goals. If we didn't truly need it, we graciously and intentionally said no.

Make a *daily* decision about what you bring into your space. You might think, *Oh, it's just a shirt, and I really need this shirt*, or, *It's just one toy that my kid will absolutely love.* You'd be surprised how much you bring into your house one item at a time and how much it adds up. How did most of us end up with full closets, garages, and basements? A semi-trailer didn't show up at my house! Stop to think about *why* you're purchasing an item, and if you really need it. Is it out of boredom? Is it just a good deal you don't want to pass up? These small steps will add up and have more of an impact on your space, your wallet, and your relationships than any discounted sweater or toy could.

Are there certain triggers for you that lead you to purchasing? After Michelle did all the work to let go of bags and bags of clothes, she would still slip and make purchases. In an effort to sustain her progress and her sanity, we looked at when she would make her online purchases and how we could break this habit. Some small steps we took were to remove her saved credit card information from her phone so she would physically have to get up and get her wallet. We also unsubscribed from most of the store emails her inbox was previously flooded with. This made is more difficult for her to go back to her old ways.

Being intentional about what comes into your house (and life) allows you to prevent returning to an overwhelmed state surrounded by stuff and clutter. It's surprising how quickly it can happen if you don't keep an eye on it. I sometimes wonder if stuff attaches to our kids' clothing or seeps in through our heating vents! Where does it all come from?

Be intentional about consuming less, and you will!

Parting Ways with Stuff (Again)

Even with the best intentions (and locked doors and blocked heating vents!), stuff will still make its way into your house. This is why I've incorporated a habit of purging regularly in our house. I encourage my clients to do the same. Once you've done an initial deep purge and have your systems up and running, it's much easier to keep up with them. But if you go too long between purge, or simplifying sessions, you'll soon find yourself overwhelmed by mounds of toys and clothes.

You can schedule these release sessions in whatever way works for you—monthly, quarterly, even just twice a year. In our house, I can just *feel* when it is time to go through a space regardless of how much time has passed. Some of my clients hire me to come to their home regularly to help maintain their systems, and we make adjustments as needed several times a year.

Whether or not you hire outside help, make it a regular event to get the broken toys, unused clothes, and other items you keep seeing (and know you won't use) out of the house. This process gets easier and easier and helps you maintain the clear space and mind you've worked so hard to achieve.

Be intentional about what you bring into your home and to move items out when they no longer serve you and you will find that your space will be much easier to maintain... and so will your sanity.

Maintaining Systems

Life is constantly changing, so our systems should adjust to accommodate this. We need to reevaluate our systems as the kids' activities, seasons, and gear changes to keep things running smoothly. To keep life as simple as possible, I look at our spaces and ask, "How can this run better?" When summer arrives and the swimming pool is the prime activity, I create a new system for swim gear. When school's out and my kids are home grabbing more snacks, I adjust our pantry for them to easily help themselves. I still hide the cookies on the top shelf—mostly to keep them from my husband! As my kids get older and can do more for themselves, we adjust our systems to allow them more independence and support. My three year old can now grab her own hat and gloves, so I find a home for these that is easily accessible for her to grab...and put away. It's a journey to keep things running smoothly and efficiently, but the payoff of having more time and energy is huge!

Take note when a system doesn't work or isn't sustainable with your family's habits or activities. Tweak your systems as needed so they don't fall apart completely. That's when some people give up and let things get out of control. If something doesn't work the first time, they throw their hands up. So don't be afraid to make adjustments. Figure out what is and isn't working. Help your kids create new habits. And know that no matter how hard you try, we are dealing with humans who get lazy sometimes. Don't give up.

Going through your spaces a few times a year and adjusting your systems as your life changes will keep things from falling apart and will help your life continue to be simpler. After all, it's Process *Improvement*...not Process *Perfection*.

Summary:

- Creating a clear, calm environment is a journey. It's not a one-and-done event you accomplish in a day.

- Just like my overall process has three steps (Simplify, Systems, Sustain), the Sustain step contains three actions: be intentional about consuming less, purge regularly, and maintain your systems.

- Be intentional about what you bring into your home every day.

- Go through your spaces throughout the year to let go of things that no longer serve you. This will keep you from accumulating stuff all over again and feeling overwhelmed by it all.

- Life constantly changes. So should your systems, as needed. Adjust your systems to make them work for your home, life, and family. It's not a one-size-fits-all approach, and it may take several iterations to get the right system for the current phase of life.

CHAPTER 8

Sanity

At the intersection of simplifying, systematizing, and sustaining is *your sanity*. Life simplification isn't about creating a perfect space.

It's about creating a space that *doesn't*:

- deplete you each time you walk into that space
- make you stressed and grumpy
- take you away from getting down and playing with your kids
- make you inefficient and ineffective in your daily responsibilities
- exhaust you by moving through your daily to-do list
- create an emotional gap between you and your partner

- throw money down the drain
- keep you from eating and exercising like you always plan

And it's about creating a space that does:

- make you feel good (maybe even smile when you enter)
- energize and motivate you to tackle the day
- allow you complete your daily responsibilities with minimal effort and time
- allow you to be more patient and present with your little ones
- bring you closer to your partner
- save you money
- give you the energy and motivation to eat well and exercise

Our world is so busy and distracting, our living environment shouldn't be. If we can create spaces in our homes and systems in our lives that allow us to slow down, be present and connect, we help our brains manage in this hectic world. We have the energy and resources to invest in ourselves. We help our kiddos become more confident, curious, and courageous. And we create a life that is more...*simplified.*

CHAPTER 9

What's Next

As you begin your own journey to simplify and slow things down in life, take a moment to look at the bigger picture for your home and life. Grab a pen and start to make some notes right here in this book!

What's your goal for your home? What does the ideal day look like?

_____

_____

_____

_____

simplified.

How does your home environment and physical space come into play with this goal. What is holding you back?

_____

_____

_____

_____

We don't eat an elephant in one bite, so make a list of the areas you would like to tackle to help you achieve this goal. Prioritize starting with low hanging fruit, one small space and working your way to the bigger, more challenging spaces.

_____

_____

_____

_____

As you go through each space, think of how you will:

Simplify - What can go and what to keep?

_____

_____

_____

_____

Systematize - Where should you put things away to make the space work best for you? What new habits can you form to allow this space to make your life simpler?

_____

_____

_____

_____

Sustain - How will you maintain order in the space? Go through things quarterly or seasonally so things don't get out of hand again. How can you adjust the space for different seasons of life.

_____

_____

_____

_____

Refer back to each section—simplify, systematize, and sustain—for more detailed steps.

Need helping getting started with this activity? Read what my client, Sara, wrote:

- *My goal for our home is to have a space that we can enjoy being together instead of always taking care of the space. Family meals used to be a favorite time of the day and I would love to have the kitchen table clear so we can eat our meals there daily and have conversations.*

- *Our kitchen table is currently covered in papers that get dropped when people come in the door. It has school papers, mail, work papers, etc.*

- *This definitely prevents us from having meals together, so we tend to eat in the living room. Then we end up watching TV while we eat and don't talk. I express my frustration with my family and then this just creates more tension.*

- *I could start by going through all of the papers to see what is landing there to figure out what we need to actually keep and what can go.*

- *Sara and I worked together to create this plan for a system: Instead of putting papers on the table, we could place a recycling bin by the front door so we can recycle junk mail right away and create a space on the table by the front door to put papers that need attention. I could also automate some bills and statements to reduce the mail coming in. Lastly, I could create a habit of going through the kids bags and school papers as soon as they get home.*

Note: for a more detailed guide on how to address paper piles, visit: www.lifemadesimpleathome.com/resources

For Sara, we realized that the kitchen table was the first area people passed when they entered the door. We started by taking inventory of all the papers to determine what was actually there. We discovered much of it was junk mail or statements that could be automated, so we worked on getting her taken off mailing lists and made most of her statements paperless to reduce the paper piling up.

We found a small empty space close to the door, and we created a drop zone with a small table and file hanger on the wall. We created a new habit where family members would drop their papers instead of tossing them onto the table to be forgotten. We also placed a recycle bin next to the table so they could quickly process the mail—recycle what they didn't need and put what they *did* need in the wall hanger for action. By reducing the overall amount of paper coming in and creating a habit of putting papers in their designated spot right away, Sara now has even *fewer* papers on the small table.

At the time I worked with Tara, it was peach season in Colorado. She and her sister have an annual peach

simplified.

jam making tradition. With the entire kitchen table covered with crates of peaches, it made it impossible for her husband and kids to pile papers there. They were immediately redirected to use the new table and filing system. The kitchen table remained clear! We made it simple for everyone to follow the system (and we left them no choice- ha!), and now they eat regular meals at the table! *Win!*

For more ideas and inspiration on how to create a more simplified life that helps you to clear your space without losing your mind, visit:
www.lifemadesimpleathome.com/resources.

Epilogue

Congrats on investing in yourself, your family and your home! I hope you found value in reading this book and picked up a thing or two that can help you in your life. Again, life simplification isn't about perfection or everything running smoothly twenty four-seven. It's about scaling back on the things in life that are not serving us and creating better systems for the things, that for most of us, we need to do every day. Running a household shouldn't drain us to the point that we have nothing left for the important moments. There are so many things in our lives to be grateful for, so let's not miss out on them.

Acknowledgements

Thank you to all of my family and friends who have supported me over the past few years!

Thank you:

To my husband for sticking by my side.

To my mother (and grandfather) who passed down the gene for organization.

To my father who taught me the value of a dollar.

To my brother for all of his tech support and being an accountability partner.

To my mother-in-law for letting me send my kiddos down to play all those afternoons so I could write.

To my friends—Bridgette, Katie and Michelle—for always supporting, encouraging, inspiring, and celebrating with me.

To Erica for connecting me with Heather and for being an amazing coach.

To Heather for teaching me so much about business and for connecting me with Joshua.

simplified.

To Joshua for being a great partner in creating this book. You have such patience!

To Sheryl, Kristen and Lindsay for being amazing women and supporting me with an abundance mindset.

To all of my clients who believed in me and allowed me to join them on their journey to live a more simplified life.

To me. For deciding to take up space with my passion and voice. Playing small never helped anyone.

Notes

Chapter 2

1. McMains, S., and S. Kastner. "Interactions of Top-down and Bottom-up Mechanisms in Human Visual Cortex." *The Journal of Neuroscience* 31, no. 2 (January 12, 2011): 587-97. Accessed November 3, 2018. doi:10.1523/JNEUROSCI.3766-10.2011.

Chapter 3

1. Sullivan, Meg. "Trouble in Paradise: UCLA Book Enumerates Challenges Faced by Middle-class L.A. Families." UCLA Newsroom. June 19, 2012. Accessed November 3, 2018. http://newsroom.ucla.edu/releases/trouble-in-paradise-new-ucla-book.

2. "The True Cost." The True Cost. Accessed November 3, 2018. https://truecostmovie.com/about/.

simplified.

Chapter 4

1. Parekh, Ranna, M.D., M.P.H. "What Is Hoarding Disorder?" American Psychiatric Association. Accessed November 3, 2018. https://www.psychiatry.org/patients-families/hoarding-disorder/what-is-hoarding-disorder.

Chapter 5

1. *180 Degrees South: Conquerors of the Useless.* Directed by Chris Malloy and Rick Ridgeway. Produced by Tim Lynch and Emmett Malloy. Performed by Yvon Chouinard and Doug Tompkins. United States: Magnolia Pictures and Red Envelope Entertainment, 2010. DVD.

2. "Ten-year-olds Have £7,000 worth of Toys but Play with Just £330." *The Telegraph*, October 20, 2010. Accessed November 3, 2018. https://www.telegraph.co.uk/finance/newsbysector/retailandconsumer/8074156/Ten-year-olds-have-7000-worth-of-toys-but-play-with-just-330.html.

3. "University of California TV Series Looks at Clutter Epidemic in Middle-Class American Homes." University of California Television - San Diego. Accessed November 3, 2018. https://www.uctv.tv/RelatedContent.aspx?RelatedID=301

Made in the USA
Las Vegas, NV
09 August 2022